A PICTORIAL JOURNEY
THROUGH
EDWARDIAN GOWER

A PICTORIAL JOURNEY THROUGH EDWARDIAN GOWER

by

David Gwynn

and

Peter Muxworthy

GOMER

First Impression — 1988
Paperback Edition — 1989

ISBN 0 86383 422 1

© David Gwynn and Peter Muxworthy 1988

Printed and Published by
Gomer Press
Llandysul, Dyfed
Wales

ACKNOWLEDGEMENTS

We would like to thank Walter Grove for permission to reproduce the photographs of Porteynon lifeboat, Marion Taylor for permission to reproduce the Duncan paintings, and Gary Joyce for assistance with research. Also we would like to thank Mrs Stanley Jones and Mrs George Edwards of Penrice for information which helped to fill some gaps and solve some problems.

PREFACE

Books about Gower appear quite frequently, but so far no book has been published which gives a pictorial evocation of Gower during one of the most interesting times in its past—the Edwardian period.

Pictorial material is more plentiful from this period than earlier eras, as the period between 1900 and 1914 was also the Golden Age of picture postcards and in this book many of the illustrations are taken from postcards. The popularity of postcards meant that many different views were published. Gower scenes were popular, so much so that a comment appeared in the Gower Church Magazine:

"It is evident from the large quantity that are seen about that the sale of Picture Post Cards is on the increase in this district.

"Visitors will be able to obtain a Pictorial Card of almost any of the parishes.

"Among the many series that are offered for sale those marked ARW and published by A R Way, Bookseller, Wind Street, Swansea are certainly well chosen and comprise views of the most beautiful spots of the Gower Peninsula.

"Strangers will be able to obtain them at most of the Post Offices in the various Parishes.

Amongst the other illustrations in this book are paintings by various members of the Duncan family. We have included these, and other drawings and photographs, as we believe them not have been published previously. Edward Duncan RWS was born in 1803, the son of Scottish parents, his father being a painter. His son Edward (known as Edward jnr) had two daughters, Muriel and Bertha, who lived at Horton, and were universally known as the Misses Duncan. Most of the watercolours we illustrate in this book are copies they made of earlier paintings by their father, or are original watercolours of their own.

LIST OF ILLUSTRATIONS

1 Map of Gower
2 The "Favourite" horse-bus
3 The "Vanguard", the first motor-bus to Llangennith
4 The "Pioneer" motor-bus
5 Gower "truckle" cart
6 Caswell Bay c. 1906
7 Caswell Bay c. 1936
8 Bishopston Post Office
9 St Teilo's Church, Bishopston—obverse of special re-opening card
10 Reverse of re-opening card
11 The Bishopston Valley Hotel c. 1910
12 Bishopston village c. 1906
13 Pwlldu
14 Kittle Green
15 Pennard Castle and Three Cliffs Bay
16 The Lodge, Kilvrough
17 Kilvrough Manor
18 Ruined Chapel, Ilston Cwm
19 The Gower Inn, Parkmill
20 Parkmill, looking east
21 The Police Station, Parkmill c. 1908
22 Parkmill looking west
23 The Mill, Parkmill
24 Penmaen Church and Schools
25 Nicholaston Church prior to restoration
26 Nicholaston Church, after restoration
27 The Towers, Penrice Castle
28 Underhill, Oxwich
29 Oxwich c. 1914
30 The Square, Oxwich
31 Oxwich Church
32 Oxwich Rectory
33 Coal boat, Oxwich Bay
34 The School and Schoolhouse, Oxwich
35 The Nook, Oxwich
36 Oxwich Post Office and Tea Rooms
37 Oxwich viewed from the New Road
38 Oxwich Castle c. 1905
39 Oxwich Green
40 Slade Valley
41 Penrice Village c. 1906
42 The Eynon Home, Penrice 1895
43 Penrice Sunday School c. 1900
44 Penrice Castle
45 King Arthur's Stone
46 The King Arthur Hotel, Reynoldston
47 Reynoldston Post Office
48 Lower Green, Reynoldston c. 1910
49 Stouthall Avenue
50 Ruins of the Church of the Three Mary's, Knelston
51 Old House at Burry Head
52 Horton Burrows
53 Horton from the beach
54 Cottages in Horton 1898
55 Pembroke Cottages, Horton c. 1898
56 Mrs Thomas and Mrs Morgan of Horton
57 An elderly member of the Gibbs family
58 Horton village c. 1908
59 The Village Pump, Horton
60 Brig-y-Don, Horton, after the fire of 1898
61 Old Well, Horton c. 1890
62 The Ship Inn, Porteynon c. 1885
63 The Ship Inn, Porteynon c. 1905
64 The Village Well, Porteynon c. 1905
65 Porteynon from beach c 1905

66 Porteynon in 1910
67 The Dell, Porteynon
68 Porteynon Quay after 1882
69 Chestnut Cottage, Porteynon
70 The Abbey, Porteynon
71 Porteynon Bay from Porteynon Point 1905
72 Salthouse, Porteynon c. 1884
73 Porteynon Church c. 1910
74 Porteynon Church with Lifeboat Memorial
75 The lane leading into Porteynon
76 Culver Hole, Porteynon
77 General View of Overton
78 The former Black Lion Inn, Overton 1890
79 SS ''Bluebell'' ashore at Washslade Bay, Overton, 1913
80 Overton c. 1904
81 The Smithy, Port Eynon 1900
82 General view of Overton 1920s
83 The smack ''Pink'' at Porteynon 1899
84 Billy Gibbs, Coxwain of the Porteynon Lifeboat
85 Porteynon Lifeboat
86 Porteynon Lifeboat
87 Porteynon Lifeboat
88 Porteynon Lifeboat
89 Porteynon Lifeboat
90 Worm's Head, Rhossilly
91 Worm's Head Cottage, Rhossilly
92 General view of Rhossilly
93 Old Vicarage, Rhossilly
94 The ''Helvetia'' on Rhossilly sands 1887
95 The remains of the ''Helvetia'' 1895
96 Middleton Farm 1884
97 Middleton—the Bevan family
98 Middleton—the Richards family
99 Sea View, Rhossilly
100 Crabbing beds, Burry Holmes
101 Llangennith Church

102 General view of Llangennith
103 The Cross, Llangennith
104 Brynteg, Llangennith
105 Broughton Farm, Llangennith
106 The King's Head, Llangennith
107 Children's Summer Home, Llangennith
108 Kennexstone Farmhouse, Llangennith
109 General view of Llanmadoc
110 The Free Library, Llanmadoc
111 Whiteford Lighthouse
112 Cwm Ivy Lane, Llanmadoc
113 Llanmadoc
114 Coal boat at the Burry River, Llandmadoc 1896
115 The Roman Bridge between Stembridge and Cheriton c. 1884
116 View of Cheriton from Llanmadoc
117 Weobley Castle
118 Landimore c. 1905
119 Llanrhidian Church
120 The Whipping Stone, Llanrhidian
121 Coal boat on Llanrhidian Marsh
122 Ploughing on Llanrhidian Marsh c. 1880
123 The Cockle Girls of Penclawdd
124 The Avenue, West End, Penclawdd c. 1907
125 Penclawdd (east)
126 General view of Penclawdd
127 Upper Killay and Fairwood Common
128 Killay hill c. 1904
129 Rev. Stephen Jenkins, Rector of Oxwich
130 Rev. Francis Atterbury Thomas, Rector of Porteynon
131 Gower costume 1900
132 Penrice Estate carpenters
133 Picnickers at Parkmill 1900
134 Edwardian tourists

INTRODUCTION

In writing about Edwardian Gower, it would be easy to describe the period as a watershed in the peninsula's history. The advent of motor transport has been credited with making a previously isolated place suddenly accessible and in the wake of this, great change was to come to Gower, which served to destroy a way of life that had survived unchanged for centuries.

Such a view, however, would be far too simplistic. Admittedly, Gower was isolated, both geographically and socially. Being a peninsula, Gower saw no through trade—it was a destination in itself, not a place on a road to somewhere else. The industrial expansion of the nineteenth century had not extended to Gower, there being no coal to exploit. Whilst much of the rest of South Wales became industrialised, Gower remained essentially agricultural.

Gower was not as remote as this picture would suggest. On the southern coast, limestone was quarried and boats carried it across to the north coast of Devon. At Porteynon, paint was mined and skiffs carried it to Cardiff for sale. It has been said that the Great Western Railway used paint from Porteynon for its livery. The people of North Gower were no strangers to South Carmarthenshire folk. At one time, so we are told, there were stepping stones from Whiteford across the mouth of the Estuary to Carmarthenshire, and it has been noted that grain from Carmarthenshire was brought across to Gower for milling.

Gower also had a number of large houses—Penrice Castle, Fairy Hill, Kilvrough, Stouthall—and to these came visitors, estate managers and workers, and they brought with them new ideas to add to the colourful Gower mix.

The seafaring tradition also added to the peninsula's outside contacts. Many Gower men became sailors, particularly on the copper ore barques which sailed between Swansea and South America. A goodly number of these Gower sailors rose to become ship's captains, and they often retired to their old villages, as men of no little wealth and immense experience. Their knowledge of foreign parts was often better than their knowledge of other parts of Gower—"I know Pennybucky (Pernambuco) better than I know Llangenny," said one.

Gower, therefore, was not as isolated as many would have thought. Whilst the majority of people never travelled very far from home, they were in contact with others who did, and these contacts meant that the changes brought about by the twentieth century were not unheralded.

Having said that, though, the Edwardian period was a period of transition for Gower. Most of the people continued to lead their lives much as their ancestors had done. Farming methods had not changed much for centuries, and the pace of life continued to be dictated by Nature. Most families grew their own vegetables, kept goats, chickens and a pig or two, and carried their water from the well or pump. The necessities of life were obtainable locally—each village had its cobbler, blacksmith, seamstress and tailor. Most villages had a post office-cum-village store where small items could be purchased—such as candles and bootblack. Luxuries were few, but perhaps the girls would buy some bows and ribbons at Reynoldston Fair each September, whilst the young men might expend some hard-earned money on a new pocket knife or some mother-of-pearl cuff links.

Farmwork continued to be hard and demanding of much human labour. In the latter years of the nineteenth century new equipment had found its way onto Gower farms—steam threshing machines, reaping, mowing and hay making machines, and traction engines. These were expensive, and were often shared amongst several farmers. Men were still needed for sowing, potato-planting, hoeing, harvesting and a host of other tasks. At the busiest times, all available hands were called on to help. School log books are full of references to low attendances due to children being kept home to help with planting or harvesting.

Leisure time was scant, but each year had its highspots. In September, there was Reynoldston Fair, to which most of Gower went. This gradually was replaced by the Gower Agricultural Society Show, as the annual Gower get-together. Even today, there are many Gower folk who look forward to the Gower Show so they can see friends they last saw at the previous year's Show. Christmas was another opportunity for high-jinks, with Wassailing, the Horses Head, the Mummers Play and holming. Each parish had, also, its Mabsant, or Saints Day. By the Edwardian period only Llanmadoc and Llangennith continued to celebrate Mabsant in the time-honoured way.

Llanmadoc Mabsant was a local affair, confined mostly to the people of the parish, but Llangennith Mabsant, held in July, had grown into a three-day celebration. Folk from all over Gower made their way to Llangennith for the fun. There was cock-fighting, fist-fighting, feasting and a whole range of other activities, most of which earned the disapproval of the Church. There were also rather more sedate pleasures—Quoits Clubs existed at Reynoldston and Old Walls, and probably in other villages, encouraged, it would seem, by the clergy, as a 'proper' outdoor activity. Schools concerts and entertainments were held irregularly, and for the schoolchildren of South Gower there were the annual treats at Penrice Castle, courtesy of Miss Talbot.

Gower had been popular with visitors before the Edwardian period. Francis Kilvert was but one eminent tourist. However, it was only the wealthy or leisured who were able to visit Gower before the turn of the century. With the advent of motor transport, travel to and within the peninsula became easier, and so began the period of mass-tourism that Gower continues to enjoy. At first the numbers of tourists were small, but they grew to quite appreciable numbers in the years just prior to the First World War.

These visitors, like those who had come before them, and those who have visited Gower since, came because the peninsula offered unsurpassed scenery, wonderful beaches and a pure charm. They saw a Gower, however, unspoilt by commercial developments—no caravan sites, chalet parks or fish and chip vans. We hope that the pictures in this book will convey something of that era.

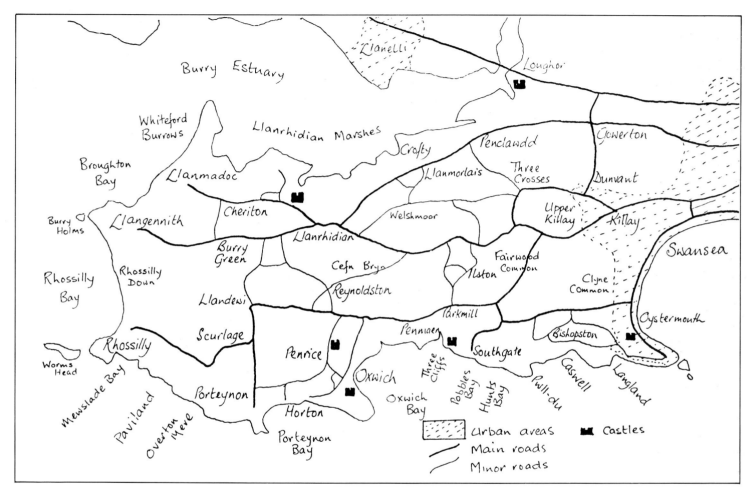

1 Map of Gower.

TRANSPORTATION IN EDWARDIAN GOWER

Edwardian Gower was not an easy place in which to travel. The roads were poorly surfaced and suffered during adverse weather conditions. Road maintenance took the form of periodic resurfacing with broken stone, but needless to say, the advent of motor vehicles caused this type of road to break up rapidly.

For centuries before the advent of motor transport, travel in Gower was by horseback, cart or on foot. The peninsula was criss-crossed by a network of green lanes, which offered direct routes between villages and farmsteads. Some of these routes became the metalled roads we use today. As motor vehicles used only the surfaced roads, so the green lanes fell into gradual disuse. This was to be a blessing in disguise, for walkers can today explore the peaceful areas of Gower by following these green lanes.

Omnibuses were not introduced until the late 19th century, when horse-buses first ran from Porteynon to Swansea. The journey from Porteynon would take about 4 hours and cost about 2/6d return. The passengers were not able to ride all the way, being obliged to get out and walk up the steeper hills. For most people visits to Swansea were rare—maybe only three or four times a year. Accordingly the most was made of a visit and each passenger would bring back quite a pile of supplies. The buses returned stacked high with a great variety of goods. Between visits to Swansea, supplies could be had by request of the horse-bus driver. Often would a request be made for the driver to bring back sheets of corrugated iron, or some other urgently needed item.

The Taylor family ran horse-buses from Llangennith to Swansea. It is said that Rowland and George Taylor's father began his horse-bus in 1896 because whenever he decided to go to Swansea, the bus from Llangennith was full. His solution to the problem was to set up his own horse-bus service. Rowland Taylor subsequently established the Swan running from Southgate, and his brother George ran the Vanguard.

At Oxwich, William Jenkins was the omnibus proprietor, and the special garaging built to house his horse-bus still exists in the village. The route in and out of Oxwich was through Penrice Park, Underhill being too steep and not properly made up. One day the horse-bus turned over, and Lottie Jenkins, who was a passenger, was only saved from being thrown out by a sack of sugar on the seat alongside her.

In 1909 John Grove introduced a motor bus on his route from Porteynon—the first motor bus in Gower. The following year George Taylor motorised his Llangennith to Swansea route. Rowland took over the route from Rhossilly formerly run by the Beynons, and brought the motor bus to Gower's most westerly village. Other services were established from other villages and by 1914 the Gower Rural District Council had been forced to introduce controls.

One story that has come down to us tells of the problem encountered in Middleton with an awkward load. A sheep-rack had been brought atop a motor bus from Llangennith or Llanmadoc, but on arriving at Middleton, it proved impossible to manhandle the

2 The "Favourite" horse-bus, which ran from Llanmadoc, through Llanrhidian and Killay to Swansea.

item from the bus. The solution was, however, to hand. The bus was driven under a tree, and ropes slung over a branch, and tied to the sheep-rack. The rack was then hoisted off the bus, which was driven out, so that the rack could be lowered to the ground. The motor buses used in Gower at this time were specially built with roof-racks to carry goods.

Most goods, however, were carried by horse-drawn wagon, with motor-lorries only gradually being introduced. Traction engines were also used to haul heavy goods such as coal, and bulky goods like hay. They were even used for furniture removal. The bicycle was a popular means of transport, and visitors from Swansea would take cycling holidays on the peninsula. The more daring young men might even have invested in a motorcycle, although the heyday of this most versatile vehicle was to come after the First World War.

The form of transport which had least effect on Gower was the railway. A branch line offering both passenger and goods services ran from Gowerton to Llanmorlais. Its effect on the peninsula was slight, although it did provide a means by which North Gower people could take their produce to market. At Gowerton this branch line brought the traveller to a minor railway metropolis. Here the Great Western Railway main line to West Wales crossed the London and North Western Railway main line from Swansea through Mid-Wales to Shrewsbury. This latter main line acted as something of a boundary between Swansea and Gower for part of its route. Between its terminus at Victoria Station and Gowerton, there were stations at St Helens, Blackpill, where the line turned inland to travel up Clyne Valley, Killay and Dunvant. Killay was the nearest station to South Gower, and many visitors alighted here in order to travel on by bus.

3 The first motor bus to Llangennith, 1910.

4 The Pioneer motor bus, which ran from Horton and Porteynon to Swansea through Reynoldston,
Penmaen and Parkmill.

5 Gower ''truckle'' cart.

A JOURNEY THROUGH EDWARDIAN GOWER

We begin our journey through Gower at the turn of the century at Caswell Bay. The boundary between the County Borough of Swansea and the Gower Rural District divided Caswell, so that the traveller on the road from Swansea entered Gower just before beginning the climb up Caswell hill.

Postcards of the period almost all show the windmill on the cliff above the bay. Built by a Mr Peek, this structure had been abandoned for some years. In 1889 it had been declared unsuccessful and had been allowed to disintegrate. Its gradual disappearance can be traced through postcards, it becoming less and less of a landmark as the years passed. By 1936, Caswell was a much busier place, with beach huts galore, but the windmill was no longer big enough to feature prominently on postcards.

With Caswell Bay behind him as he climbs up the hill, the traveller enters a land of fertile fields and magnificent vistas. At Bishopston, evidence of the productive nature of Gower's soil could be seen all around. This was a village of market gardens—Swansea's larder—with fruit and vegetables being grown for sale at Swansea market.

The church at Bishopston underwent two restorations—one in 1851, and a second in 1927. It would seem that the 1927 restoration removed various of the 'improvements' of 1851. The Edwardian visitor would have viewed a church internally quite different from the one to be viewed today. The church reopened after the second restoration with a special service on 28 July 1927.

Bishopston village stands at the head of Bishopston Valley. The stream which runs down the valley disappears partway down into a hole called Guthole, and reappears further down the valley. Our Edwardian visitor may have been fortunate enough to have witnessed an incident here which has been passed on to us by oral tradition. The weaving of cloth was carried out at Bishopston (indeed blankets woven there in the last century are still in use in at least one Gower home), and it was customary to wash the cloth in the stream. One day, around the turn of the century, a piece of cloth of particularly good quality was swept along by the stream. Its owner sent a boy after it. The cloth, however, disappeared into Guthole, and the boy was sent down to retrieve it. The cloth re-emerged farther down stream, but the boy had become stuck in the cavern and had to be rescued.

Had that piece of cloth been washed downstream, it would have been taken out to sea at Pwlldu Bay. This bay is quiet now, but up until the first years of this century it was a hive of bustling activity. The quarry here produced limestone, for export to the west of England, and there were a number of houses and at least four public houses here. Today only scant remains of the quays exist, but in Edwardian times the quays would have been all but complete, having only just been abandoned. Unfortunately, they do not show up on contemporary postcards. Quarrying took place on the cliffs of many Gower bays, and the marks of this industrial activity can still be seen. The quarrymen made 'slides' down the sides of the cliffs. The quarried limestone was brought down these slides on sleds, and at the bottom, was loaded into boats.

Travelling westward from Bishopston, the traveller would endure an uncomfortable climb up to Kittle. The old road between the villages zig-zagged up the steep valley side. Edwardian Kittle was a tiny hamlet, and very few postcards of it exist. The one illustration we have shows a pleasant pastoral scene on the edge of Kittle Green. Bishopston can be seen in the background.

Beyond Kittle, the road meandered through the scattered farms and houses of Pennard. Here the visitor would have made a point of visiting Pennard Castle, perched high above Three Cliffs Bay. This Norman castle has always been surrounded by legend. Its abandonment is explained as a fairy curse. The Edwardian visitor to Gower may well have read this version of the legend which appeared in the Gower Church Magazine: ''Here (at Pennard) in the days of old, lived a bold and hardy chieftain, whose martial fame resounded far and wide throughout the land. Hard by, in houses clustering round the castle, of which all traces have long since disappeared, dwelt his band of trust warriors, who attended their liege on the battlefield whensoever he desired. Oft he would lead them forth against some neighbouring foe; and as often would return victorious at their head, and laden with the spoils of war. It chanced upon a time that a Prince of Northern Wales had a quarrel with his neighbour; and, aware of the Pennard Chieftain's prowess, sought his aid against his foe. Forth from the battlemented archway passed the doughty warrior with his men to aid the Northern Prince. The fight was long and fierce; but in the end the Prince and Chieftain rolled back the tide of war; and the grassy sward was deep-dyed with the crimson stain of blood. When the fight was won, the Prince enquired of the chief what he deemed a fit reward for the service he had rendered. 'Thy daughter's hand in marriage,' was the reply. 'Twas hard to grant; 'twas dangerous to refuse; so, summoning his fair daughter to his side, he asked her if she would consent to be the bride of him who helped to win the fight, and thrice had saved her father's life upon the battlefield. Timidly she gazed at the grim warrior who sought her hand, in whose eyes the fierce glare of battle had given place to the soft sweet glance of love, and murmured low, 'I consent to be thy bride'. He clasped her to his heart; forthwith a trusty herald was despatched to announce the speedy home-coming of himself and his bride; and in a few short days the wedded pair arrived beneath the grey walls of the castle looking down upon the sea.

''That night within the castle walls was heard the sound of mirth and feasting. The wine-cup passed from hand to hand, and shouts and laughter made the walls of the old castle ring again. Outside the moon and stars shone brightly down. The sentinel paced to and fro upon his lonely beat, hearing only the sounds of revelry within, and the soft murmur of the waves upon the shore. It was the hour of midnight. Suddenly a strange sound fell on his ear. He paused to listen. He looked around. From the grassy dell below there floated upward to the castle walls a soft sweet melody, answered by a chorus as of angels. Such bewitching strains he had never heard before. He roused the warder. Together they listened to the wondrous music. They called the chieftain. Flushed with wine, he came forth to listen; and with a rude, rough oath swore to end the music. Down the sandy height on which the castle stood he and his followers strode on to the grassy dell beneath. There, in the moonlight, they beheld a company of elves disporting themselves, whirling round and round in mazy dance, and making the air throb with their wondrous harmony. Laying about them with their swords, the chieftain and his men rushed into the mystic circle, vowing destruction to the fairies. But what could vulgar weapons of steel do against such airy, impalpable foes as these? Mad with rage and disappointment the chief was about to make his way back to the castle. Just then a low sweet voice was heard which said, 'Rash chief! Rudely hast thou distrubed our revels. In vain thou seekest to destroy us. We are proof against thy steel. And, for thy rash intrusion, this shall be thy doom. Thy proud fortress shall become a ruin, and the homes of these thy warriors shall be seen no more.'

"Scarce had the voice ended, when in the distance a dark cloud came driving up the channel, then another, and another, and another. Faster and faster, thicker and thicker they came, till the air was filled with choking sand, and moon and stars were blotted from the firmament. And soon the proud battlements looked down upon a scene of devastation; and the homes that clustered round had disappeared beneath the sand.

"That night, they say, from some spot in Ireland, a huge mountain of sand suddenly and mysteriously disappeared. How, whither, and by whom it was conveyed away, none could ever tell. But the grey old walls, and silent heaps that stand around—and they had tongues—perchance could solve the mystery."

The road from Pennard to Parkmill cannot have changed much in the 85 years that have passed since the dawning of this century. It may now have a sound surface, but it is as narrow as ever it was, as modern motorists passing Kilbrough will testify. In the Edwardian period this imposing house was the home of Thomas Penrice, and consequently was of great local importance. Today the house is an outdoor pursuits centre run by the Oxfordshire Education Committee, but in outward appearance neither the house nor the Lodge have altered much.

Parkmill was a place of some importance. Here could be found a sawmill, school and police station, and here the traveller could slake his thirst at the Gower Inn, and buy postcards to send to friends. In Ilston Valley, a visit could be made to the ruins of the earliest chapel in Wales, built by John Myles in 1649. At the western edge of the village, above the mill, in Green Cwm, our traveller could see Giants Grave, a Stone Age burial site, and a popular subject with Edwardian postcard publishers.

Beyond Parkmill, the road brings our traveller to Penmaen, with its picturesque church, and dominated by the Gower Union Workhouse. Below Penmaen, at the mouth of the river which runs through Parkmill, lies Three Cliffs Bay. This distinctively picturesque bay is dominated by Pennard Castle, and has always been popular with visitors.

At Nicholaston, the traveller passes the isolated church of St Nicholas. This church has the dubious distinction of being the most heavily restored of any church in Gower. The church that the Edwardian visitor saw bore no resemblance to the same building of only 30 years before.

At the Towers, the traveller could choose to divert from the main road and visit Oxwich. Oxwich, like Pwll-du, was a limestone quarrying and exporting village. The quarries on the cliffs beyond the church produced large quantities of limestone, and the bay was busy with the small boats which carried coal in and limestone out. The area where the quarrymen worked had, some hundreds of years ago, been the site of part of the village, but erosion had caused the buildings to disappear into the sea. The last to fall to the power of the sea was the old rectory which disappeared at the end of the eighteenth century. A new rectory was built a little further inland.

From the Cross at Oxwich, our traveller could take the hill called the New Road to Oxwich Green, passing Oxwich Castle on the way. Originally built during the Tudor period as a fortified manor house, part of the building had been converted into a farmhouse, whilst the remainder was allowed to fall into ruin.

Beyond Oxwich Green, the lane terminates in the hamlet of Slade, at the top of Slade Valley.

Inland from Oxwich lies the village of Penrice. At one time this was the most important village in Gower, with a twice-weekly market and a fair four times a year. However, by the Edwardian period, the village had declined and had become a quiet backwater. Up until the early years of this century, a house with a low-walled garden stood on the green between Church Cottage and the church itself. This house, which we know only as ''the Eynon's home'', was demolished before 1908. A Duncan painting of it survives, and shows it to have been a typical Gower cottage.

Penrice village also boasted a purpose-built Sunday School, which stood to the south of the church, on the opposite side of the green. A footpath led across the green so that the scholars could make their way unhindered from church to Sunday School on a Sunday. It is quite likely that the Sunday School fell into disuse during or shortly after the First World War.

Although Penrice village had become a much less important place than formerly, Penrice Castle continued to be the seat of the most influential family in Gower—the Talbots. During the Edwardian period the house was occupied by Miss Talbot. Most of west Gower was owned by the Penrice Estate, so her influence was considerable. It would seem, though, that Miss Talbot was a benefactress too, for there are many instances on record of her distributing prizes to schoolchildren at Oxwich, Porteynon and Rhossilly schools, and also she laid on an annual treat for these same schoolchildren. Penrice Castle, at this time, comprised the Georgian mansion built c. 1775, to which had been added a large extension during the Victorian period. The Talbot family was an important one, and there were many visitors to Penrice Castle, including the King himself on 20 July 1904. This Royal visit was the cause of much interest in Gower, and was even reported in the Gower Church Magazine:

''The peninsula of Gower and more particularly the parish of Penrice, was honoured on July 20th by a visit from His Most Gracious Majesty King Edward VII. His Majesty drove out from Swansea in his motor car, and arrived—preceded by Mr Andrew Fletcher in his motor car—at Penrice Park a little before half-past five in the evening. Miss Talbot kindly allowed the children from the school, and all her workmen with their wives and families, to assemble inside the Park, where they were able to see his Majesty and give him a good hearty cheer on his arrival. His Majesty took tea at the Castle, and afterwards planted an oak tree in the Park. He then drove to Oxwich sands returning in Miss Talbot's carriage, after which he again took his seat in his motor car and returned—once more amidst the heartiest cheers of the Gower people—to Swansea. This is the only visit of a king to Gower of which we have any record: but we are quite sure that his Majesty has no more loyal subjects in the whole of his great empire than in this peninsula.''

Oxwich Bay is dominated on the landward side by Cefn Bryn, the long hill which effectively separates North and South Gower. A little inland from Penrice the western slopes of this hill drift gradually down to the village of Reynoldston. Our visitor would not miss the opportunity of walking up to the top of Cefn Bryn and there view one of Gower's most famous landmarks—King Arthur's Stone. This large stone stands on a number of smaller stones, with a slice of the larger stone lying alongside. The origin of the stone is lost—though much speculation has taken place concerning its purpose. Most likely it marks the burial place of an important early British chieftain. Needless to say, lack of knowledge about the stone has led to many legends growing up concerning it. One states that King Arthur was riding from the Battle of Camlan when he felt a pebble in his shoe. On removing the stone, he threw it, and when it landed on Cefn Bryn, it grew to its present size. Another legend states that the stone goes down to the Burry Pill to drink on the nights of a full moon. Yet another legend gives the stone the power to determine true love. It is said that if a girl wishes to

determine the faithfulness of her young man, all she need do is place a cake on the stone at midnight, and walk around it three times. If the young man appeared, his intentions were true, but if he failed to show, then he was false.

The flat piece of stone lying alongside the Stone is also the subject of legend. Many Gower folk believe it was chiselled off by a miller, who wished to use it for a millstone, but found it unsuitable. However, there is a legend that St David himself struck the stone with his staff, to prove to the pagan natives that their gods were false. The result was the sundering of the stone. Which story is true we cannot tell, but the stone must have been split before the sixteenth century, for the writer Camden makes mention of it at that time.

At Reynoldston the traveller could refresh himself at the King Arthur Hotel, and spend a little time in this centrally-placed village, before resuming his coastal journey at Horton.

On his way to the coast, the traveller's route skirts the grounds of another of the great houses of Gower—Stouthall. Like Kilvrough, Stouthall today is owned by an English education authority—the London Borough of Merton—and it is used as an outdoor pursuits centre. At Stouthall can be found a pillar, sometimes referred to as a Celtic Cross, but when it was painted by the Duncans, it was described as the burial place of a horse.

A little further along the road from Reynoldston to the coast, lies the small community of Knelston. Here the visitor could view the remains of the Church of the Three Mary's, which had fallen into disuse in the fifteenth century. Beyond Knelston, the road takes a southerly turn at the village of Llandewi. This village, like Penrice, was once of great importance, but had declined to become a quiet backwater. In the Middle Ages, the village contained a number of important houses, including a Palace of the Bishop of St Davids.

Edwardian Horton was much smaller than the present-day village. At best it would have been described as a hamlet, yet its growth over the 75 intervening years has probably been greater than any other village in west Gower bar Reynoldston. Horton is situated at the eastern end of Porteynon Bay, with Porteynon itself at the western end. In Edwardian times Porteynon was one of the busiest of Gower's villages. It was a limestone quarrying centre, fishing village and the home of the Porteynon lifeboat. Towards the point, the visitor could view the quay, and the remains of Salthouse. These ruins are all that remain of a house, probably the home of a fishing family. This house was certainly occupied in the 1860s, as there exists a Duncan painting showing not only the house, but piles of fishing tackle outside. This Salthouse was not, however, the original Salthouse.

In the fifteenth or sixteenth century John Lucas, son of David Lucas of Stouthall, appeared to be a ''wild spirit: he was lawless and wild spirit, albeit a young man of fine and bold front, and very comely to the eye, and brave like a lion.'' He quarrelled with his father, and left home going to ''divers strange countries, where he was brigand and pirate, beyond the law.''

After some 9 years, he returned, and was reconciled with his father, who built for him a residence at Porteynon called 'Salte House'. However, the isolated position of Salthouse, and the opportunities presented there, proved too much of a temptation for John. He fortified the house, and began a life of smuggling and wrecking. The stories of John Lucas also credit him with fortifying 'Kulverd Hall' (Culver Hole), although this is by no means certain. He was ruthless in his illegal activities, and he was not averse to killing shipwrecked sailors who resisted his wrecking operations. He was, however, popular locally, giving aid to the poor. Rather boringly, for such a colourful character, John Lucas settled to a law-abiding lifestyle as he grew older, and died peacefully. His mansion was eventually destroyed in the great storm of 1703.

Porteynon's greatest claim to fame is perhaps the heroism of her lifeboat crew and the disaster which overcame the lifeboat in 1916. On January 1st of that year, the SS Dunvegan came ashore at Oxwich. The lifeboat from Porteynon arrived at the scene, but the crew had already been taken off by the rocket company from the shore. The lifeboat turned to make her way back to Porteynon but the gale was so strong and the sea so high that she was overturned and three of the crew lost. Those three were the Coxwain, Billy Gibbs, Second Coxwain William Eynon and lifeboatman George Harry. The remaining crew were able to right the boat and made for Mumbles, where they arrived the following day. The bodies of William Eynon and George Harry were recovered and are interred in the churchyard at Porteynon. The lifeboat was never replaced at Porteynon, the whole of the Gower coast being served thenceforth from Mumbles. A public subscription resulted in a memorial being placed at Porteynon Church. The Edwardian visitor to

Gower could well have witnessed lifeboat practice at Porteynon, and there are a number of postcards and photographs of the lifeboat in existence.

Above Porteynon, our traveller could have made a detour to Overton, a small hamlet overlooking Porteynon Bay.

From Porteynon, the road westward to Rhossilly brought the traveller to Gower's western extremity, to Worm's Head. This magnificent promontory, which retains to this day its Viking name, has appeared on countless postcards. It is perhaps the abiding image of Gower. Very occasionally views of the Worm from the seaward side can be found, and they show vividly how rough the seas here can be in this most exposed expanse of water.

Rhossilly itself stands on the cliff above the southern end of Rhossilly Bay. Being isolated it too had a reputation for smuggling and wrecking. By the beginning of the century, though, travellers enough were making the journey to Rhossilly to view the rugged scenery that tourism began to replace these older, more traditional activities. Evidence of the involvement of the whole community in smuggling can be found at the old vicarage, along the bay. Just behind the house were built hiding places for the contraband brought in at dead of night.

The journey by road from Rhossilly necessitates retracing one's steps as far as Scurlage, and then going through the lanes of Burry to Burry Green and thence to Llangennith. The more intrepid foot traveller, however, could walk along Rhossilly Bay, eventually reaching Burry Holmes, and the village of Llangennith beyond the sand-dunes.

Llangennith has been referred to by some as the most typically 'Gower' of all Gower villages. The truth of this statement might justifiably be challenged by some other villages, but Llangennith's isolation certainly gave the village a character of its own, and afforded the villagers a feeling of independence. It is told that during the First World War, when daylight saving measures were introduced, the villagers of Llanagennith met to decide what they were going to do. Eventually it was decided that they would give the new system a month's trial to see if it suited them! Presumably it did, as nothing more was heard of the matter.

Llangennith was an important religious centre in the early Middle Ages. In the sixth century St Cennydd founded a monastery and college on Burry Holmes, and the foundation survived into the sixteenth century. Llangennith Church, the largest in Gower, is testimony to the importance of Llangennith as a religious centre. Llangennith was also the home of Phil Tanner, the last of Gower's true folksingers. Coming from a family of weavers, he married the widowed landlady of the Welcome to Town Inn at Llangennith. Much of his time was spent on odd jobs around the village, and he would often be heard singing as he worked. He was a bit of a rogue, and there were some who disapproved of his approach to life. He was, though, a masterly singer, and could be relied upon to provide songs at village functions. His talents also stretched to mouth-music, and he could maintain a lively dance tune for some time, with no instrumental assistance.

The most north-westerly village in Gower is Llanmadoc, and like Llangennith its relative isolation gave it a character all of its own. Llanmadoc Church is the smallest in Gower, and during the Edwardian period its incumbent was the Rev J D Davies, who was a historian and scholar, and who recorded much of Gower's history and legends. Modern historians owe him a great debt, for much would have been lost but for his meticulous work. Beyond Llanmadoc, stretching into the Burry estuary, lies Whiteford Burrows, with Whiteford Lighthouse perched at its most northerly point.

Returning from Llanmadoc, the traveller would follow the road down into Cheriton Valley, through the tiny village of Cheriton. This village, too, has a connection with the Lucas family. Representatives from the Porteynon branch of the family once fought with those from the Stouthall branch in the churchyard here. The rector of the parish at the time was a Lucas relative, but the combatants locked him in the Church, so that they would not spill blood in front of a clergyman. The north coast of Gower looks out over Llanrhidian Marsh towards the Burry Estuary. Near Landimore, Weobley Castle stands sentinel, with views across to the Carmarthenshire coast. Our Edwardian traveller may well have visited this remarkably well-preserved Tudor fortified manor.

The village of Llanrhidian was a relatively peaceful agricultural village in Edwardian times. The visitor would certainly have toured the church, and wondered at the 'Whipping Stones' which stood on the green outside the gate. Were people really tied to these stones and whipped as a punishment?

The road from Llanrhidian to Penclawdd ran across Llanrhidian Marsh, which meant that at high tide travellers were forced to wait for the waters to recede. The line of the road was marked with wooden posts so that those venturesome souls who insisted on making their journey when the water was over the road, would be able to see its line.

At Llanmorlais industrial Gower really began. Our Edwardian traveller could board a train here, which would take him to Gowerton, via Penclawdd. He would also see coalmines here, and at Penclawdd there was a tinplate works and more coalmines. This was a different Gower—a Welsh Gower—with customs and traditions quite unlike those of agricultural peninsular Gower.

Penclawdd was, of course, the home of the cockle industry. Even in Edwardian times the village was famed for its cockle-girls, who went out onto the Marshes to dig for the shellfish delicacy. Some did not return for the hazards were many, and the waters of the Burry Estuary were not always considerate of those who fished there. On more than one occasion a brave, laden pony dragged both itself and its exhausted mistress to safety through the swirling waters.

From Penclawdd our traveller could choose to go on to Gowerton—by road or rail—or he could take a route up to Blue Anchor and Three Crosses, to arrive at Upper Killay, the other gateway into Gower. In the Edwardian period, Upper Killay consisted only of a few scattered farmsteads, although by the 1930s residential developments began to push the urban fringe of Swansea further towards Fairwood Common. Just as Caswell on the coast saw the boundary between Swansea and Gower, so here between Upper Killay and Killay, the boundary was formed by the railway which ran from Swansea Victoria, through the cutting here, to Gowerton and thence to mid-Wales. Once over the railway bridge, our traveller was in Killay, his journey through Gower over.

6 Caswell Bay c. 1906 showing the windmill on the clifftop.

CASWELL BAY (1.) SWANSEA

7 Caswell Bay c. 1936. The windmill is no longer visible.

8 Bishopston Post Office.

9 St Teilo's Church, Bishopston shown on a presentation card issued on the occasion of the re-opening of the church after restoration in 1927.

10 Reverse of the presentation card shown in Plate 9, giving details of the re-opening service, and a plea for further financial assistance.

RE - OPENING SERVICE

(AFTER RESTORATION)

By the Right Reverend the

Lord Bishop of Swansea and Brecon.

THURSDAY, JULY 28th, 1927, at 3.0 p.m.

Still Wanted ! £500. *Please send your contribution to the Hon. Treas. (Miss Morgan, Caswell), or to the Rector.*

11 The Bishopston Valley Hotel c. 1910.

12 View of Bishopston village, showing the church and school, c. 1906.

13 This view of Pwlldu was taken after 1932, and shows a quiet bay with none of the bustle of fifty years earlier when the limestone quarries were in full operation.

14 Kittle Green, with Bishopston in the distance. This view probably dates from about 1903.

15 Pennard Castle and Three Cliffs Bay.

The·Lodge, Kilvrough Gower.

16 The Lodge, Kilvrough, near Parkmill.

17 Kilvrough Manor.

18 Ruins of the first Baptist Chapel, in Ilston Cwm.

19 The Gower Inn, Parkmill, with the school in the background.

20 Parkmill looking east, showing the Gower Inn. The bridge in the foreground crosses the river which flows down Ilston Cwm and meets the sea at Three Cliffs Bay. This early twentieth century view shows a wooden bridge, which was later replaced by a concrete structure.

21 The Police Station, Parkmill c. 1908.

22 View of Parkmill, looking west.

23 The mill at Parkmill c. 1920. The village name Parkmill is derived from the fact that the manorial mill of Parc le Breos was situated on the river here. The mill shown in this picture, however, is a sawmill not a flour mill, so is not the original mill which gave the village its name.

24 Penmaen Church and schools c. 1910. The school was finally closed in 1944, having been used for evacuees during the Second World War.

Nicholaston Parish Ch.
prior to Restoration

Geo. E. Halliday del
1892

25 Nicholaston Church prior to its restoration. Sketch by Geo. E. Halliday, 1892.

26 Nicholaston Church, after its restoration. Comparison with the sketch in Plate 25 shows how much the work altered the structure.

27 The Towers, Penrice Castle. Although they have the look of genuine Norman ruins, few people realise that the gateway is a folly.

28 Underhill, Oxwich.

29 Oxwich c. 1914. The building on the extreme left of the picture is the school, and on the extreme right are the Coastguard Cottages.

30 This view is described as ''The Square'', Oxwich, and would seem to have been taken at a busy time!

31 St Illtyd's Church, Oxwich. This view, dating from around 1905, shows a part of the wall below the Church, which has since disappeared. The sea continues to eat away at the land here, and it is only a matter of time before the church is seriously threatened.

32 Oxwich Rectory.

33 Coal boat, Oxwich Bay. Boats bringing in coal and taking out limestone were beached and whilst the tide was out, unloaded and reloaded. The boat would be refloated when the tide came in again. This undated sketch was made from an older sketch by Edward Duncan Jnr.

34 The School and Schoolhouse, Oxwich.

THE COTTAGE IN WHICH
JOHN WESLEY SLEPT. — OXWICH.

35 The Nook, Oxwich, famed as the cottage in which John Wesley stayed during his visits to Oxwich.

36 Oxwich Post Office and Tea Rooms. This Post Office was opened in 1901.

VIEW OF OXWICH

37 Oxwich viewed from the bottom of the New Road to Oxwich Green.

38 Oxwich Castle, viewed from the west. At this time (1905), part of the building was in use as a farmhouse.

39 Oxwich Green—The Row.

40 Slade Valley c. 1906, when the valley was sparsely populated.

41 This view of Penrice Village, taken from the top of the 'Mount', the Norman earthwork which dominates the village. From the evidence in the picture, it would seem to have been taken after 1905. The Eynon house, painted by the Duncans, has gone, but the new wall built in its place is bright and obviously only recently erected.

42 The Eynon Home, Penrice. Painted by M. Duncan, from a photograph taken by Dr. Clark of Gloucester in 1895.

43 Penrice Sunday School c. 1900.

PENRICE CASTLE.

44 Penrice Castle—with the Norman castle in the background and the Georgian mansion in the foreground.

ARTHUR STONE

45 King Arthur's Stone, being viewed by some Edwardian tourists.

46 The King Arthur Hotel, Reynoldston.

47 This rather unusual view of Reynoldston shows the Post Office and the chapel. Titled "St. George's Road, Reynoldston", it is not clear to which road the title refers. The church at Reynoldston is dedicated to St. George, so possibly the name derives from that connection. The road leading away from the photographer leads to the Lower Green, and the church is adjacent to that.

48 Lower Green, Reynoldston c. 1910.

49 Stouthall Avenue, on the main road from Swansea to Porteynon. The gateway into Stouthall itself can just be seen on the right hand side of the picture.

50 Ruins of the Church of the Three Mary's, Knelston, by M. Duncan.

51 Old House at Burry Head, by W. W. Goddard.

52 A view across Horton Burrows, with Porteynon Point in the background.

53 A view of Horton from the beach, probably taken just before the First World War.

54 Cottages in Horton 1898. Outside the left hand cottage is Mrs. Thomas ("Nellie") and outside the other cottage is Mrs. Morgan ("Nanny").

55 Pembroke Cottages, Horton c. 1898. Sketch by M. Duncan.

56 Mrs. Thomas ("Nellie") (left) and Mrs. Morgan ("Nanny") (right) of Horton.

57 An elderly member of the Gibbs family.

58 Horton village c. 1908 by M. Duncan.

59 The Village Pump, Horton.

60 Brig-y-Don, Horton, after the fire of 1898.

61 Old Well, Horton by W. C. Goddard c. 1890.

62 The Ship Inn, Porteynon, A copy by M. Duncan of a sketch made by Allan Duncan in 1885.

63 The Ship Inn, Porteynon, with a sign above the door proclaiming the landlord to be H. Hughes. This view dates from the early 1920s.

64 The Village Well at Porteynon
c. 1905.

65 View of Porteynon from the top of the beach c. 1905.

66 Porteynon in 1910, viewed from the hill above the village.

67 The Dell, Porteynon. Painted by M. Duncan in 1947, but showing the house as it had been for many years.

68 Porteynon Quay after 1881. Copy by M. Duncan of a sketch by Allan Duncan.

69 Chestnut Cottage, Porteynon (demolished 1956).

70 The Abbey, Porteynon. When pulled down in 1952, this house was reputed to be 800 years old.

71 Porteynon Bay from Porteynon Point 1905. Some activity can be seen around the quays on the left hand side of the picture.

72 Salthouse, Porteynon c. 1884, by Allan Duncan.

73 Porteynon Church, dedicated to St. Catwg, c. 1910.

74 Porteynon Church, photographed after 1916, and showing the memorial to the lifeboatmen who lost their lives in the lifeboat disaster of that year.

75 The lane leading into Porteynon.

76 Culver Hole, near Porteynon. Legend credits John Lucas of Salthouse with the fortifying of Culver Hole, which he then used for his smuggling activities. Alternatively, it may have been a pigeon loft, as the inside of the wall does have niches similar to those found in pigeon houses.

77 General view of Overton, probably painted by Edward Duncan Jnr.

78 The former Black Lion Inn, Overton, 1890. The occupants at the time were the Roberts and Eynon families. The building was demolished in 1898, just before the Edwardian era.

79 The SS ''Bluebell'' ashore at Washslade Bay, Overton, February 13th, 1913.

80 Overton c. 1904—watching the chickens!

81 The Smithy, Porteynon, 1900

82 Overton viewed in the 1920s. Few postcards exist of Overton, as it was not one of the villages much frequented by tourists.

83 The smack "Pink" discharging coal at Porteynon, 1899.

84 Billy Gibbs, Coxwain of the Porteynon Lifeboat, with a group of young men, outside his cottage.

85 Porteynon Lifeboat, on the sands.

86 Porteynon Lifeboat, with crew, horses, and onlookers.

87 Porteynon Lifeboat, with crew and small boys.

88 The Porteynon Lifeboat being pulled out to sea by its team of horses. This particular boat, called ''A Daughter's Offering'', was in use between 1888 and 1909.

89 Porteynon Lifeboat and crew outside the Lifeboat Station.

90 Worm's Head from the sea.

91 Worm's Head Cottage and Worm's Head, Rhossilly.

92 General view of Rhossilly.

93 Old Vicarage, Rhossilly.

94 The "Helvetia" on Rhossilly sands
1887.

95 The remains of the "Helvetia", 1895.

96 Middleton Farm, 1884.

97 Postcards often feature groups of people posing for the photographer. Sometimes they are incidental to the scene, but sometimes their presence turns an otherwise ordinary postcard into an important item of local social history. This view shows a farm at Middleton, near Rhossilly, and features a number of people. Some we have been able to identify: on the extreme right, wearing the straw boater is Alf Bevan, with Annie Bevan in the doorway of the house. The little girl sitting on the wall above the cow's head is Ada Bevan, with Ruth Bevan behind her, and 'Mother' Bevan (Jane) is standing behind the wall with her back to the lean-to. On the extreme right, holding two ponies, is Ingram Chalk, and the bearded man in the background holding the horse is Edward Beynon. The others have not been identified.

98 Middleton, Rhossilly. Another Gower family appears in this postcard—the Richards. One of the two boys standing together in the road is Ernest Richards.

99 Sea View, Middleton, Rhossilly, just after the First World War. According to the sign, H. Williams, Grocer, ran a shop here.

100 Crabbing beds, Burry Holmes.

101 Llangennith Church, the largest of Gower's churches.

102 General view of Llangennith.

103 The Cross, Llangennith

104 Brynteg, Llangennith.

105 Broughton Farm, Llangennith.

106 The King's Head, Llangennith, showing the piped spring in the foreground. This view was probably taken after the First World War—notice the petrol pump outside the pub.

107 Children's Summer Home, Llangennith.

108 Kennexstone Farmhouse, Llangennith. The building was taken down in 1952 and re-erected at the Welsh Folk Museum, St. Fagans.

109 A general view of Llanmadoc taken from Cheriton. The pub below the road in the foreground is the Britannia.

110 The Free Library, Llanmadoc. This was situated near the Britannia, and can be seen on the general view in Plate 109, about halfway up the hill.

111 Whiteford Lighthouse, situated at the most northerly point of Gower.

112 Cwm Ivy Lane, Llanmadoc.

113 Copy by M. Duncan of a drawing of Llanmadoc made by Allan Duncan c. 1890.

114 Coal boat in the Burry River, Llanmadoc 1896. Copy by M. Duncan from a sketch by Edward Duncan Jnr.

115 The Roman Bridge, between Stembridge and
Cheriton, c. 1884, before the traction engine
"Jumbo" went over it and broke down the central
arch. Copy by M. Duncan of a sketch by Edward
Duncan Jnr.

116 View of Cheriton, from Llanmadoc.

117 Weobley Castle, near Llanrhidian.

118 Landimore c. 1905.

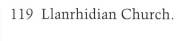
119 Llanrhidian Church.

120 The Whipping Stone, on the green outside Llanrhidian Church. It is said that miscreants were chained to this stone, and whipped, as a punishment for their misdeeds.

121 Coal boat on Llanrhidian Marsh by Allan Duncan.

122 Ploughing on Llanrhidian Marsh c. 1880.

123 The cockle girls of Penclawdd, with their donkeys, baskets and sieves.

124 Penclawdd—the Avenue, West End, c. 1907.

125 A view of the east end of Penclawdd showing the tinplate works.

126 A general view of Penclawdd, probably taken just after the First World War.

127 Upper Killay—a group of motorcycle enthusiasts gather on Fairwood Common near Upper Killay.
This photograph was probably taken in the early 1930s.

128 View of Killay hill, taken from the railway bridge, c. 1904.

129 Rev. Stephen Jenkins, Rector of Oxwich until 1918. He had a reputation throughout Gower as a spellbinding preacher. Worshippers would arrive early to be sure of a seat at his services. Often the crowds would fill the churchyard—and at Penrice on more than one occasion, spilled onto the green.

130 Rev. Francis Atterbury Thomas, Rector of
Porteynon 1914-1953. Although suffering
from a stammer, the Rev. Thomas was a
much respected man.

131 Gower costume as worn by some elderly Horton ladies at the turn of the century.
Back (l to r): Mrs. Betty Rees, Mrs. Roberts (nee Nicholas).
Front (l to r): Mrs. Phillips, Mrs. Thomas ("Nellie"), Mrs. Morgan ("Nanny"), Mrs. Nellie Bevan (nee Rees).

132 Penrice Estate carpenters c. 1902.

133 Picnickers at Parkmill 1900, watching one of their number dancing—it must have been some picnic!

134 Edwardian tourists, probably at Porteynon. It is rare to see such an informal photograph from this period.